Nu
For Sale

J. Matton

J. Matton

Copyright © J.Matton 2015
All rights reserved

Nu For Sale

This is a work of fiction and any resemblance to people, living or dead, is purely coincidental. The idea to write this story derives from the countless instances of actual crimes committed against humanity. Many such occurrences still pass unnoticed or ignored around the world today in one fashion or another.

J. Matton

Dedicated to all the victims of human traffickers and innocent children of the world.

Contents

Chapter 1
Vinh Chau, Viet Nam

Chapter 2
New Country

Chapter 3
Northern United States

Chapter 4
The Homecoming

Other Books

Chapter 1

Vinh Chau, Viet Nam

"You can't even make your first payment. I demand the money now or I will take your house and land. It will be mine." Mr. Nygen said to Yen about the loan he gave her a few weeks before.

"The fishing has been very bad and my boat needs repair. Somebody damaged it. I've been sick. I have no money for you today and I need more time!" She angrily replied. "You told me you would be flexible with the payments."

"No, your time is almost up. Have the money in five days or you have to be out of here, understand? Do you understand?" He repeated before heading for the door. As Mr. Nygen was leaving, he glanced around the property imagining all the things he could do with it or how much he could get when he sold it. He was counting on Yen not being able to pay him the money she owed so it would belong to him.

Yen, her daughter, and brother did not have anywhere to move to if she lost her house. Her brother, Danh, could not work making things worse. He had recently lost his leg in an accident. They needed the house to have a place to live. Otherwise, they would be living on the street. Danh happened to be coming home as Mr. Nygen was leaving. He was in his homemade wheelchair.

"I hate that man. What did he want?" He asked his sister.

Yen told him everything and he understood how serious the situation was. "I've been looking for work but there is none available anywhere for a man with only one leg. I would help with money if I could."

"We are going to lose the house. We won't have anywhere to live." Yen said as tears began flowing down her cheeks.

"I think he's the one who damaged your boat. I saw him near it the day it happened and he has no business being down there. He doesn't own a boat!" Danh suddenly remembered something one of his friends told him. "There are people looking to hire laborers to work in factories in Ho Chi Minh City and other places. They like to hire children and pay lots of money up front. The children work and repay the loan."

"No, no! Nu is only eight and a half. She's too young to go to the city to work." Yen replied. She thought about it for a few minutes. She looked around her house and her property which she had worked hard all to life to acquire. If she lost it she didn't know what they could do or where they would live. She soon realized her brother's idea was her only choice.

"Alright, I'll talk with her tonight and see how she feels about it."

Danh left to ask his friend to get in touch with the men from Ho Chi Minh City. Later that evening, after his friend called them, he set up a time to meet with them. They would come to her house and talk with Yen. Two days later, they arrived and looked Nu over closely. "She'll do fine." One of them said. "She'll be thoroughly trained and will earn money enough to pay back the money we will give you today."

Nu realized she was the topic of the conversation and something was wrong. She understood she was going to have to leave with the strange men and began crying.

"I don't want to go with you." She told them. Yen was ready to change her mind until one of the men reached into his pocket and pulled out an envelope full of cash.

"Here's five thousand dollars. Yes, five thousand dollars like we said. It is all here. If you accept this money in exchange for your daughter, you will then be able keep your house and have your boat fixed. She will go to work in a restaurant or factory after she is trained and we'll bring her back when the loan is paid off." He handed the envelope to Yen.

Yen had never seen so much money at one time in her whole life. She quickly stuffed the money in her purse. Her house was safe from Mr. Nygen now. She could pay him, have the boat fixed, and maybe have enough money left over to bring electricity to the house.

The men took Nu by the hand to their van. She did not want to go but stopped resisting after her mother said they could keep the house if she went to work for a little while. Nu waved good-bye to her mother as the van pulled away. Yen suddenly had a sinking feeling deep inside her stomach. She was not sure she had done the right thing. She was worried about Nu and already missed her. She hollered for the van to stop, but it was too late. It was already gone.

The men took Nu to a temporary waiting place in Ho Chi Minh City and pushed her into a room with twenty other young girls. She looked around the dimly lit space for a place to lie down but there was not enough room. A woman then came into the room. She told all the girls they had to wait until everyone arrived and at that time, their new jobs would be ready.

"Your new jobs have been delayed because of a small problem. Meanwhile you can work around here to help pay your expenses. It cost a lot to feed you, you know, so you must work to pay for it and to payback your loan. I am your *mamasan*. You may call me madam if you want."

The girls looked at each other in puzzlement. They did not know what to think. One of them asked, "What will we do here? Cook, clean, sell, or what?" A week passed and nothing happened. Nu waited along with the other girls. They took turns lying down to sleep. They were fed them one meal per day consisting of rice and chicken and a bottle of water. One evening the *mamasan* returned and handed each of them a numbered tag.

"Stick these numbers onto your shirt right here." She pointed to her front left shoulder. "And follow me."

She led the girls into a different small room inside the building, one that they had never seen one before. There were a few decorations on the wall and a handful of chairs. The bright red decorated walls possessed many shiny ornaments and a large oriental light fixture. There was a curtain covering a wall-sized window on one side.

"Find a place to sit." The *mamasan* ordered them before she left to go into the next room.

The taller girls sat in the chairs and the rest sat on the floor. After a few minutes, the curtain opened revealing a large glass window. They room on the other side of the window was not well lit but they could see into it. Inside the room, they could see tables with men sitting around them drinking beer and whiskey.

The men suddenly looked up at the girls as the curtain opened. A few were smiling. They stared intently.

Nu had a bad feeling. She knew this was not going to be good. As the young girls whispered to each other, the men wrote on note pads. Occasionally one would signal the *mamasan* and point at one of the young girls. The *mamasan* would record the tag number of the girl at which he was pointing. Nu was one of the prettier ones. She watched in horror as the men drank and gawked at her. A minute later another woman whom they had never seen before opened the door and called out numbers. Nu's was one of them.

"When I say your number, you must come with me." She said.

The girls whose numbers were read reluctantly stood up and slowly walked toward the door.

"Hurry, I say, hurry! Don't dawdle."

Nu For Sale

Nu was the last in line. The woman looked at her and smiled. "You were the first one chosen. You're the lucky one."

"Chosen for what?"

"To do your duty. You might even be the first girl to get her loan paid back within five years."

Nu almost started crying. *Five years. I can't want to stay away from home for five years.* She did not understand how long five years was but knew it was a very long time.

The girls were separated and led to separate small, dimly lit rooms. Nu's room had a small bed with a dirty sheet covering it. Next to it was a small table with several little packages. Nu picked one up and looked at it but did not understand what it was. The walls were a pinkish color with little flowers painted on them. There was a fan sitting in one corner and a washbasin on one side. She noticed there were no windows. She sat on the edge of the bed and waited even though she did not know what she was waiting for.

A few minutes later, the door opened and an old man walked in. He was scruffy looking and smelled as if he had not bathed for a long time. A grey beard growth covered his dark brown face and his decayed yellow teeth protruded outwards. Nu heard the door lock behind him as he moved into the little room and stood in front of her.

"Take off your clothes," he said sternly.

"No!" Nu replied.

"I said take off your clothes!" He reached down and slapped her on the head.

"No!" She yelled.

That made him angry. "I paid good money for you, now take off your clothes or I'll hurt you!"

He pushed Nu back on the bed and started tearing her clothes. He ripped her shirt in half and pulled her arms out of it. He then pulled off her pants and tossed them across the room. Now Nu was naked lying on the bed in front of a strange man. She screamed causing him to press his hand over her mouth. Unable to breathe easy, she started crying as he removed his trousers and knelt on top of her. It hurt her as he went inside her. He pressed his hand even harder over her mouth as he raped her. Only then did he notice the condoms on the bedside table.

"Oh, I forgot to put on a condom. See what you made me do?" Nu did not say anything. She only laid there crying and wincing in pain. "Don't tell *mamasan* I didn't use a condom, okay? If you do I'll come back and really hurt you bad."

Nu quickly wrapped herself in her torn clothing. He dressed and left the room.

Later the *mamasan* came in and looked in the empty wastebasket. She then counted the condoms on the table.

"What's this? He didn't use a condom?"

Nu still did not say anything. She only sat there staring at the walls.

The *mamasan* hollered through the doorway. "Stop that man!" She then looked at Nu. "Go back to your room, take a shower, get some new clothes, and come back. You've got more work to do tonight."

Nu returned to the girl's room while the *mamasan* changed the bed sheet now stained with Nu's blood. On the way to the girls room Nu heard some shouting and looked up in time to see the man being beat over the head with a rattan cane. The employees were forcing him to pay more money for not using a condom.

In the girl's room little Nu cried. She did not understand what just happened to her. She was in pain. Through the closed door, she heard the *mamasan* call her name telling her to hurry. She quickly showered and changed clothes. Within minutes, she was back with the other girls wearing her number. Her number was soon called again.

Nu passed out after the fifth time being with a man that evening. The *mamasan* looked her over. "You are done for now," she said. "That's enough for your first day."

As the days passed, the *mamasan* increased Nu's workload to a point she could not take it anymore. Her health was failing and she was almost unable to walk.

One day the *mamasan* noticed strangers being curious about the establishment and asking questions about the place. Some were foreigners of western descent. She notified the owner of the place who became very nervous upon hearing the news. The owner knew the end was in sight for his business and he must either move or close his door permanently. He chose the latter. He placed several phone calls to his associates, one of who was a human-trafficker. He decided to sell the girls to him. When they were sold, they would be delivered to dealers overseas. His problems would then be gone along with all the evidence. Meanwhile, the girls will go to an underground facility to await their destiny.

Late one evening a few days later, everything was ready. The two strangers who took Nu from her home in Vinh Chau drove the girls to a secret entrance at the Container Freight Station Warehouse at Ho Chi

Minh Port. There were several security guards waiting for them. They counted the girls and then delivered them to a special container ready to be loaded onto a ship. The drivers paid off the guards and drove away.

Inside the container, there were bunk beds but not enough for all the young girls. There were also large bottles of water and baskets of food. In one corner was a toilet box with a lid. Nu saw several small holes for ventilation near the ceiling. Before closing and locking the metal door, one of the guards brought in a box of jars filled a red liquid.

"If you want something to help you sleep and pass the time away, drink a little of this each day," he said to the group. "Oh, and do not scream. Do not make any noise at all. If you do I will come back and shoot all of you."

This scared all the young girls. One of them asked where they were being taken.

"To your new homes. It will be okay, don't worry." The guard answered.

Nu began crying again. She wanted to go back to her home with her mother. Now she knew she was going far away. She believed she would never be able to go home again. They huddled together and waited. Later that night they heard something attach itself to the box they were in and lift. They were jostled around for twenty minutes until the shipping container was placed onboard a large containership. They listened as the box was fastened down and another one set on top of them. There was not anything they could do except wait.

Chapter 2

New Country
During their first week on the ship, most of the girls suffered from seasickness to a point it became unbearable for everyone. The poor ventilation was a health hazard and there was no place to dispose of the waste. The group of children was nothing more than human cargo in the worst imaginable conditions. One girl died after four days and two more after the first week. Their bodies soon began to decompose and smell. They could feel the ship dock at several destinations and each time they believed their ordeal was over, they only unloaded some of the containers and go back to sea again. At each port, several of the girls banged on the sides of the container and yelled as loud as they could. Their voices were too weak and the area outside was very noisy and no one could hear them.

The three-week long trip across the ocean was extremely miserable for them. Many of the days were very hot and the nights chilly. The ship rocked back and forth and during one particularly bad storm, it felt like it was going to tip over and sink beneath the waves. Only each time the ship would slowly right itself.

Finally, it was time to remove them from the container. Twenty-four days had passed and most of them could not last one more day inside the box. They felt the ship dock and the container on top of them lifted. A few minutes later, they felt their box being raised and moved to a flatbed truck. The dockworkers then secured the container and the truck drove away. Next, they were on the highway for over three hours. The girls believed their ordeal would soon be over when they felt the truck backing up onto a dock and the seal on the door removed. The doors finally swung open. The men standing there quickly covered their noses and began spraying the inside of the container with water. Several of them bent over and vomited from the smell that rushed out of the container through the open doors.

The girls were in such bad shape they could not even enjoy the fresh air. They had blank stares on their little faces and were too weak to stand. They had to cover their eyes from the bright sunlight after many days inside the dark container. The men sprayed the container and wearing boots, gloves, and mask, entered and one by one. They carried the girls out of the box and to a warehouse where a doctor was waiting.

The doctor quickly examined them and did what he could to help. They were nourished through IV tubes and needles but one more died regardless. Over half of the children had perished during the voyage.

They stayed in the warehouse under the doctor's care until they were strong enough to move again. One day, several more men and one woman came to the warehouse to look them over. They were taking notes. They pointed at each of the girls and talked among themselves. Next, they separated the remaining girls into two groups and placed into utility vans for transport to different receiving points. None of the vans had windows in the rear. Each one had a driver and one extra person to share the driving and keep an eye on their cargo.

They were on the road again. The van Nu was riding in travelled for ten hours with only a few brief stops. She and the other girls slept most of the time.

At one point, the driver of Nu's van began cursing as he slowed down and pulled off to the side of the road. "Damn, we are almost there too." He turned around and told the girls to be very quite or he would cut their tongues out. A highway patrol vehicle with flashing lights pulled them over. The driver told the girls not to make a sound and to cover up and hide. There were two cops approaching the van one on each side. Nu could see very bright flashing lights in the rear view mirrors.

The driver and one of the cops exchanged a few words while the other cop shined a flashlight into the back of the van.

"What are you carrying in there?" he asked. Then he saw a small pair of eyes. "Is there somebody inside the back? Everyone, please step out of the van!

The men, not wanting their operation exposed, were beginning to panic. They looked at each other and at the same time reached for a handgun hidden beside their seats. In unison, they pointed the guns at the cops and fired. The girls screamed. The men then sped away as fast as it could go. "Shut up back there or we'll shoot you too."

"We have to get rid of this van. They had a video camera in their car." One of the drivers said.

"I know, but first let's deliver our cargo then we'll get rid of it." The other driver replied.

A few miles along the road, the van turned onto a narrow dirt road. It came back after a few minutes onto a different highway leading to a large city. The van meshed into the heavy traffic and another fifteen minutes they were in the city. They finally stop in front of a large building. In front of the building were several high-end nightclubs. One of the men stepped out of the van and unlocked the door on the building. He then pushed open a door large enough for the van to drive though. A minute later, the van was inside the building.

The girls were ushered out of the van and led to a brightly lit room. In the middle of the nicely decorated room, there were several tables surrounding a bar. On the tables were baskets of fresh fruits and soft drinks and bottled water. Many sofas lined the walls. The drivers ordered them to sit and wait. A few minutes later the woman they had seen before came into the room. She took the girls, two at a time, into a separate room with a shower and new clothes. She told them to freshen up and change into a pretty dress. Afterwards, she led them to a make-up table where someone was waiting to comb their hair and apply make-up.

After all the young girls were prepared, they returned to the brightly lit room and told to wait again. A man brought a television set into the room for the girls to watch as they waited. Only a few of them had ever seen one.

Later that evening men began arriving and sat around the bar and at the tables. They stared at the girls. A man and a woman came in and told all the girls to line up along one of the walls. The man then said something none of the girls understood.

"Let the bidding begin."

One by one, each of the girls stepped forward as the men began bidding on them. When the bidding stopped, the girl was to stand next to the man with the highest bid.

Nu suddenly felt very sick. She was too weak to stand and fell to the floor. The man left and a few minutes later, a different man came into the room, picked her up, and carried her away to an isolated room. "You're no good to anyone now," he told her after looking her over carefully. Soon after, other people came into the room.

Nu could hear them talking to each other. "We're going to have to get rid of her. She can't work anymore, not even as a maid." One of the men said.

"We've got to do something quick," another one who acted like a senior member of the group spoke up. We have been here at the same place for too long and ICE agents are beginning to snoop around asking questions. Today is our last day here. All the girls are going. I don't care where they go, just get rid of them. You know what to do.

The man who made the winning bid received his money back and left to bid on other girls as Nu was loaded into a van. They covered her with blankets and drove outside of the city and into the countryside.

"Where are we going to do it?" The driver asked the man sitting next to him.

Just then, Nu began crying. The men turned around and looked at her. "Be quite back there kid." The driver ordered.

The other man started at her battered body. He had been in the business for a long time and had become callous to the job and the things he had to do. Nu was just another body to him, something inhuman. Alternatively, something that could be treated as property and even killed. However, Nu was suddenly bringing emotions to his thoughts. He began to feel sorry for her. All the horrible things he kept hidden somewhere in his mind of the things had done to the little girls was surfacing and troubling his soul.

"Do we have to do this? Really? Why don't we, for once, just let this one go? Release her."

"What? Are you crazy? The boss would kill us."

"C'mon. Are you scared of the boss that much? He'll never know. Besides, I think the operation is in its last days. It's going to be shut down and man are we in trouble when that happens. The boss will rat on us to save his skin, you know that."

"Well, what are we going to do? Just pull over and throw her out on the highway?"

"No, there is a forest about an hour up ahead with lots of little cabins. We'll find a place in there to release her. Maybe someone will take her in and adopt her."

"But there's wild animals in the forest and it's wintertime you idiot. She'll die there anyway."

"At least she has a chance. Let's take her there. I won't do the other thing this time."

"Well, we have to stick together no matter what. Alright, where is the forest?"

An hour later, the van turned off the highway and on to a small dirt road leading into the forest. The men saw isolated areas and a few cabins. Some appeared to be occupied full time. They drove for another hour and saw the perfect spot. They lifted Nu out of the van, carried her to a small clearing near an old cabin, set her down on the ground, and quickly departed. They could hear dogs barking as they turned the vehicle around and drove out the same way they came in.

J. Matton

Chapter 3

Northern United States

Thelma glanced out her window at the dogs. *Hush! Hush already!* She said to no one in particular as she peered out her window.

The dogs always barked before nightfall to announce to any predators in the woods that they were now on heightened sentry duty. They usually stopped after a minute or two but on this evening, they continued their ritual causing Thelma to grow impatient. She was growing tired waiting for the noise to cease. She finally wrapped her robe around her frail, aged frame and unlocked the front door as she tightened her lips to display her anger. She swung open the heavy wooden door, stuck her head out the opening, and yelled.

"Be quite already!" The dogs were incessant and would not cease, however.

She felt a chill on her uncovered ankles as an icy cold wind blew snowflakes inside the cabin. She noticed a strange rhythm to the barking. One, which she had never heard before. It was not the normal sound, which the dogs usually made before nightfall. Nor was it a barking designed to scare someone away. It was more of an alert. She closed the heavy wooden door and turned around.

"Carl, go see what the dogs are barking at. They won't shut-up. It might be that old fox trying to get in the chicken coup, or maybe another bear!" She returned to the kitchen area in the small cabin to tend a brewing pot of stew.

Carl was sitting in his padded chair while listening to a local weather report on the radio. "Just a minute, there's something in the air. Maybe that's what the dogs are barking at."

"Something in the air? You don't need no weatherman to tell you that. Look out the window. It's snowing!"

He listened closely for a few more seconds to the broadcast indicating a major winter storm approaching the area. He then begrudgingly pressed hard on his knees and managed to stand up as he reached over to switch off the radio. The years were catching up to his frail body that now seemed to creak with every movement. His age-spotted arms and legs didn't move as quickly and sure as they use to do.

"Alright, I'm going."

He wrapped a warm overcoat over his shoulders, slid his stocking feet into his boots, and headed for the doorway. "Wait, did you say bear? I better take the rifle just in case." He grabbed his Marlin 30/30 and carefully stepped outside onto the porch. Snowflakes slapped him in the face. The dogs were still barking. He balanced himself on the icy porch while surveying the clearing in front of the cabin. The sky was dimming as the storm grew in intensity. There were streaks of amber mixed in low cloud layer moving over the area. Limbs of the tall conifers were bending at steeper angles as the wind grew stronger. Snow was already beginning to accumulate into drifts making travel difficult.

The dogs were still barking and scurrying around a small pile of debris half way to the tree line. Carl did not notice it earlier that day. He looked closely at the pile and saw what appeared to be some clothing. It was moving.

What the hell is that? That ain't no bear!

Thelma hollered from the kitchen as she huddled near the fire under the kettle. "Hurry up and close the door. I'm freezing in here."

Carl turned to face her. "Remember that car we heard a short while ago making its way through the woods? Looks like they dumped something."

"Well, go see what it is and close the door!" *I hope it ain't another dog. We can't take care of what we got now!*

With the rifle under one arm, Carl closed the door behind him and stepped off the porch. As he made his way to the pile of debris, he could hear a faint whimpering sound. The closer he was to it the louder it became. The snow almost fully covered the pile.

"Get back," he ordered the dogs as he approached it. He leaned over. "Let's see what is making that noise." He brushed off the snow and peeked under the loose clothing. He was startled to see a small pair of dark eyes staring back at him.

"Lord have mercy!"

Suddenly he heard a scream. Carl stepped back. It's okay child, you're safe now. Nothing's going to hurt you."

The screaming quieted only a little but the whimpering continued. The dogs were finally quite again. They had notified their master of the pile containing a small human.

Carl uncovered the little body and picked it up. "Why, you're a little girl. What are you doing alone out here in the woods?" She did not speak. He carried the child back to the cabin and held her up to his wife. "This was what all the fuss is about." He lay her down on the sofa and then returned to the spot to retrieve his rifle as his wife examined her.

"Oh, my! What on earth? How did you get here? Look at you, you're freezing and starving." Thelma wiped of the little girls face and sat her down. She covered her up with a blanket then poured a little stew into a cup and began spoon-feeding her. The little girl only ate most of the stew in the cup, curled up in the chair and quickly fell asleep. She could sense that she was now safe. Her tiny lips, still purplish from the freezing air, puckered as they blew the cold air out of her lungs. There appeared to be several bruises on her face.

Carl came back into the house and walked up to Thelma. "What do you think happened to her? She looks like she was badly abused. Whoever was driving that vehicle must be responsible."

"I don't know. I'll take care of her now. She's my gift from heaven!"

"You can't just keep her like she was a stray animal. We better call Sheriff Rutherford." He reached for the receiver and held it to his ear.

"I know, but we can wait until after the storm and nurse her back to health and *then* call the sheriff." Thelma said before he began dialing.

"I suppose we can do that."

Thelma stared at the little face. The little girl was sound asleep. Her long, black hair covered her eyes. Thelma put her hand on her face.

"She's still cold. Carl, put some more wood on the fire. She looks Asian doesn't she? Maybe Chinese, or something."

"Carl glanced back at her as he lifted another log to throw on the fire. "She looks Filipina to me. I was in the Philippines during the war, you know."

"You can't tell me that! You know the war was already over when you were there."

"Ha, just seeing if you were listening!"

"Carl, what are we going to do with this child? I want to keep her."

"I'll wait and call the sheriff in the morning. We ain't got no phone service now anyway. The line's dead." He said as he picked up the receiver to test the line.

"Oh dear, we must to get her to a hospital Carl," Thelma said as she peeked under the child's clothing. "She's got bruises all over her. Who could of done this to her?"

Carl did not hesitate. With a flashlight in hand, he made his way to the barn and pried open the large wooden door. He then drove his old pickup truck out of the door a few feet but the rear wheels began spinning in the snow. He gave up and returned to the cabin.

"We ain't going nowhere in this mess. It's too deep now. We're stuck."

"In that case, we'll just have to keep her comfortable for now."

As Carl and Thelma ate their supper, the child slept. She slept most of the night but woke up once crying. Thelma comforted her best she could until she fell back asleep.

The morning arrived after a long and cold night. Carl was up most of the night feeding logs onto the fire. The storm was worsening and all the windows were cover with snow and ice. He found a clear spot on one of them and peered out of it towards the barn. All he could see was the side of a large snowdrift. He then donned his heavy coat, boots, and snow pants and walked towards the door.

"I'm going to shovel some snow and clear a path.

"Okay Carl, I'll get breakfast ready."

The little girl woke up as Thelma prepared eggs, bacon, coffee, and toast. Thelma held a glass of goat's milk it to the little girl's lips. She quickly drank the liquid.

"There now, that's better. Do you have a name?"

A soft, faint voice came out of her mouth. "My name is Nu."

"I'm Thelma, that man who just left was Carl, my husband. Where did you come from? How did you get here?"

"I don't know. Some men took me to a place where other kids were and we were all put in a big box and loaded onto a ship with many boxes. There were tiny holes in it and I could see out a little bit."

"Oh, dear child. What happened after that?

However, Nu was very weak and before she could answer, she drifted to sleep again.

"Sleep for now child and when you wake up breakfast will be ready."

Carl shoveled snow away from the barn until he was able to drive the truck out of it. He stopped in front of the cabin and went inside just as their morning meal was ready. Nu was awake again and already eating. He checked the phone again but the line was still dead.

"The sun's out now and I think we can make it into town. We'll take her to the general hospital."

At the hospital, the doctor performed a thorough examination. Upon completion, he turned to the duty nurse. "We have to notify the authorities. She's been severely abused."

"She's lucky to be alive," the physician stated. "What a tough little thing. It is a good thing you brought her in when you did, although. She has pneumonia and is almost dead. But I think we cave save her."

The authorities came and assessed the situation with the abandoned little girl. They left her at the hospital for treatment and when she regained her health, they began questioning her. Nu told them everything she knew. Until they could find her a home, they gave Carl and Thelma Johnson temporary custody of her knowing they would take good care of until a more permanent home could be found.

However, Nu missed her mother and her country. She wanted to go home. She told everyone she met that she was worried about her mother and uncle. Her caretakers agreed to try to locate them and let the courts decide what was best for her.

Chapter 4

The Homecoming

Yen was sitting alone on her front porch staring at the road one evening. She was sad and confused as to why she could not locate her daughter. The men who took her away could not be located. Her brother tried unsuccessfully to locate them or Nu. Yen now realized she had made a mistake in letting Nu go with them, even if it meant saving their house. She missed her daughter terribly. It had been over a year since she had last seen her. She had paid back the loan from Mr. Nygen and had her boat repaired. Fishing was good once again and all she needed now was her daughter returned home. Everyone she had contacted about her knew nothing of what happened to her or the location of the men from Ho Chi Minh City.

One of Yen's neighbors saw her on her porch and approached her. When Yen told her she was thinking about what had happened to her daughter, he decided to help.

"I can drive you to the city tomorrow and you can go ask about her at the Ho Chi Minh City Police Headquarters if you want. They might know something. You might have to pay them a little bribe money although."

"Really? You will take me there?"

"Yes, in the morning. I'll get my car ready and we'll leave tomorrow morning."

The next day Yen arrived at the police department and was able to talk to someone about her daughter. When she told them her story, the officer left for a few minutes, and returned carrying a large file.

"Come in to my office, please. This is all the information we have on human racketeers in the city."

Yen follower the woman into her office and sat opposite of her.

"I am in charge of these types of crimes. Your daughter's name was familiar to me. You see, we received a call from the United States the other day."

"Crimes?" Nu interrupted. "What do you mean? My daughter was only going to work, in a restaurant or something."

"Your daughter was forced to work as a prostitute in a brothel. We shut it down, but not before they were able to smuggle all the girls out of the country. She was kidnapped and taken away to work in another country. We didn't know where until the call came."

"What call?" Yen inquired.

"It was from an agency in New York City. They have your daughter and want to know about you and why you sold your daughter."

"I didn't sell her. Well, not exactly. I want her back, please. It was a very big mistake."

"We can request that she be returned to Viet Nam. Nevertheless, you must go to court and start the proceedings there. It is all very expensive; however, the good news is she can be returned to you if you convince the court. Another bit of good news is there is an agency in the U.S. willing to pay all your expenses. They want to see your daughter rejoined with her natural mother. Your daughter misses you, it seems."

"Oh, dear, I want that more than anything in the world. Please let it happen! I will never let her go away again."

"Well, in that case, I have something else to tell you. You will be going to the U.S. to pick her up pending the court's approval. The same agency in New York offered to pay your expenses for that also.

After all her paperwork was finalized the courts had agreed that it was best for Nu if she was reunited with her natural mother as soon as possible. She then boarded a flight and flew to the U.S. to pick her up. Nu was waiting for her at the airport. Also present were Carl and Thelma who still had Nu in their custody. Nu ran to her mother and hugged as hard as she could.

It was sad for Carl and Thelma to have to let Nu go away from them but knew it was for the best. They were too old to raise a child and an isolated cabin was not the best place for her, they believed. The next day they met again one last time when mother and daughter returned to Viet Nam.

The End

Other Books

PROXIMITY
Conor moves Singapore to start a business escorting cargo ships through the pirate-infested Malacca Strait. However, fate intervenes one day when he meets a rich, young Filipina girl who lost her papa and best friend when pirates attacked their yacht in the Sulu Sea. Desiring revenge against the pirates, she asks him if he can help her find them and have them punished. The story is set in many exotic places around the world. 233 pages.
http://amzn.com/B00D4SBZFO

Jason's Magic Sail
Jason escapes his studies by falling into a dream world. He is then magically taken to different islands in his little sailboat by a seagull that lives in one of his library books. He discovers the world can be a dangerous place and studying isn't so bad after all. 25 pages.
http://amzn.com/B00XT17W2G

Airports
East vs. West
What is wrong with airports across the USA today? Why is the TSA out of control and expanding to our highways and elsewhere? This story compares Los Angeles International Airport (LAX) to Suvarnabhumi International Airport (BKK) and how each copes with the modern security required in today's world. One of these airports treats its users with a high degree of respect while maintaining peace and order while the other one has fallen to the bottom of ratings in customer satisfaction. This book attempts to answer these questions and offers ways to make commercial flying enjoyable once again. 86 pages with photos.
http://amzn.com/B00N89F4GA

Stickyrice and Sourmangos
American Undercover Agents in SE Asia
Together with his partner, Mark, known as Stickyrice, and John, known as Sourmangos, risk their lives hunting international criminals in Thailand, Cambodia, and China. Based on a true story. 110 pages.
http://amzn.com/B00NJUJQHQ

www.ingramcontent.com/pod-product-compliance
Lightning Source LLC
Chambersburg PA
CBHW021001180526
45163CB00006B/2462